Contents

Walk

1. The Bestwood Ramble			
2. Hunger Hill Circular			
3. The Risley Round			
4. The Elvaston Circular			
5. The Three Woods Walk	5.3	10.1	2-3
6. Cossall, Strelley & Babbington Walk	6.4	10.3	3-4
7. The Two Canals Circular	6.5	10.5	1-2
8. The Mapperley Round	7.2	11.6	4
9. River Trent View Circular	8.8	14.1	2-3

Walking times shown are approximate and depend on fitness, weight of rucksack, weather, conditions underfoot and height climbed.

Level of Difficulty 1 = Easy, **3** = Moderate, **6** = Hard
All walks are shown on O.S. Explorer map No. 260 Nottingham. Every effort has been made to ascertain the accuracy of the walks described. The description of a route or track is not necessarily a right of way.

Every effort has been made to ascertain the accuracy of the walks described. The description of a route or track is not necessarily a right of way.

Some abbreviations have been used in the text to shorten it and make it more concise: -
M = Metres **km** = kilometres **°M** = magnetic

Walkers are strongly advised to have the appropriate clothing and footwear for these walks.
• Boots/walking shoes.
• Waterproof Jacket.
• Over trousers.
• Small Rucksack for food, drinks and spare clothing.
• Hat & Gloves.
• Compass & map.

ISBN 978-1-903568-52-1

Walk 1 The Bestwood Ramble   **Distance** 4 miles/6.5 km
Start GR. 551481 'The Spinney' Cul-de-Sac, opposite the entrance to
Bestwood Country Park Mill Lakes sign.
Walk Time 1 hr 50 mins
Terrain A pleasant walk through woods and over fields with only a few
slight ascents/descents and some nice views over large areas.

Leaving the junction of the B683 at the corner of 'The Spinney'
cul-de-sac (1), walk along the cul-de-sac to the far end and look for a narrow
opening between the houses on the far side. Follow this a short distance to
where the path divides at the corner of some modern houses and turn left.

Ascend the path keeping the fields on your left then descend to a kissing
gate. Go through and head across the field in the direction of a large
house (old rectory) in the woods ahead. Go through another two
kissing gates to emerge on an access road. Turn left on the road and walk on the
road to pass the old rectory on your left (2).

Continue along the road through the wood then after 380m you come to
Alexandra Lodges, a large building with an archway where the road runs
under. Just as you reach it, take the path to the left, which ascends the hillside
(called Colliers Path), but not the one to the far left by the fence.

You come to an access track with a farm off to your right. Turn left
here and walk for 1km, passing a mushroom farm (3) and emerging at
Killarney Park residential area. When you reach it, turn left to descend
the road through the park and continue to the bottom. Look for the
yellow/green arrows on the post, for Robin Hood Way at the bottom, pointing
left along an access track.

Follow the winding access track past the farms and houses walking
anti-clockwise for approx 1km to the entrance to Goosedale
Conference Centre (4) and ahead now on Goosedale Lane to the main B683
road. Turn left at the main road and walk south for 1km with care back to where
you started at 'The Spinney'.

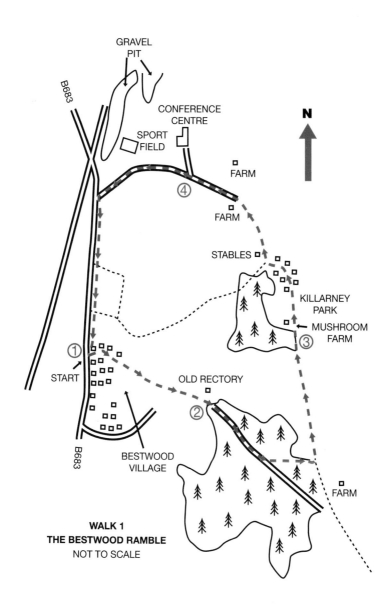

GRAVEL PIT

B683

CONFERENCE CENTRE

SPORT FIELD

④

N

FARM

FARM

STABLES

KILLARNEY PARK

① START

MUSHROOM FARM ③

OLD RECTORY

②

BESTWOOD VILLAGE

B683

FARM

WALK 1
THE BESTWOOD RAMBLE
NOT TO SCALE

Walk 2 Hunger Hill Circular   **Distance 5 miles/8 km**
Start GR. 604449 Park in Kingsbridge Avenue at Arnold, just off B684
Walk Time 2 hrs 35 mins
Terrain A nice walk over fields with good views and only small ascents/descents.

Leaving Kingsbridge Avenue, turn left to walk to a public footpath sign pointing to Lambley on your right, just past the farm shop near the junction with the B684 (**1**). Cross the stile and follow the path across three fields and at the far end is a yellow arrow on a post. Turn right, to walk along the edge of the next field keeping the hedge line on your right.

Continue over several fields in an easterly direction with the hedge line on your right. You come to a divide in the path and a yellow arrow. Bear right and continue with the hedge line on your right. You walk through Lambley Dumble (**2**) and as you approach the school through an opening into a playing field, cross it diagonally left to an opening in the hedge line, cross the concealed stile and ascend the hillside to the right of the houses.

Emerging on the road at the top in Lambley, turn left in front of the houses for 150m then cross to a public footpath over a ladder stile (**3**). Descend the field, turning left then right to cross a footbridge at the bottom. Go through a kissing gate then ascend the field, crossing a stile. You pass Jericho Farm on your right as you cross several stiles before emerging on the minor road.

Continue straight ahead, descend then ascend the road for 700km, passing a row of cottages on your right. At the sharp bend at the top, turn left (**4**), cross a stile then go straight ahead, do not turn right here. Cross several fields keeping the wire fence to your right.

Cross two stiles at the far end as you still keep the fence then the hedge on your right. You come to a bridleway going left to right, turn left and walk between the trees for 300m to the entrance to Lambley House Farm. Turn right then immediately left, crossing a small footbridge. Descend the field, keeping the hedge line just to your right.

Descend then ascend several fields in the same direction following the yellow arrows on posts and keeping the hedge line on your right. At the top of the field you come to a copse where you turn left following a public footpath sign and descend the field.

Continue to an opening halfway down then turn right along the next field, keeping the hedge now on your left. Walk for 350m before turning left, right then left following yellow arrows through two kissing gates. Ascend to the minor road (**5**) and turn right for 180m to a kissing gate on the left side.

Go through the kissing gate, turning right in the field then left, to descend the field south for 700m in a straight line to rejoin your original path. At this point, the worn path bears right (**6**), retracing your steps to emerge on the road at the junction near to where you started. Turn right here to walk back 300m to your original starting point.

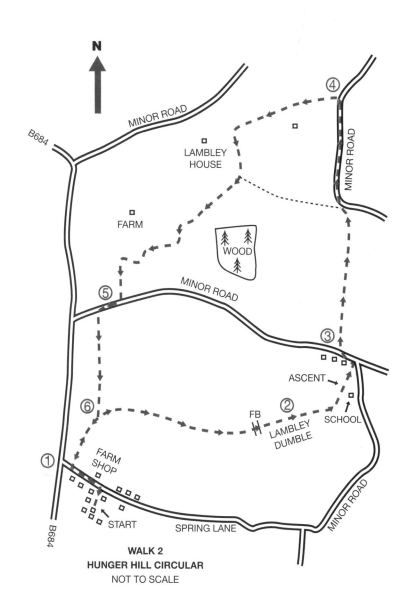

N

MINOR ROAD

B684

④

LAMBLEY
HOUSE

MINOR ROAD

FARM

WOOD

MINOR ROAD

⑤

③

ASCENT

② SCHOOL

⑥ FB

LAMBLEY
DUMBLE

①

FARM
SHOP

B684

START

SPRING LANE

MINOR ROAD

WALK 2
HUNGER HILL CIRCULAR
NOT TO SCALE

Walk 3 The Risley Round   **Distance 5.6 miles/9 km**
Start GR. 458356 The Risley Park Pub.
Walk Time 2 hrs 30 mins
Terrain A nice walk on access tracks and over fields, with opportunity for refreshment at the start/finish and ¾ of the way round.

Leaving the Risley Park pub (**1**), cross the main road and walk initially on a concrete then dusty access track/bridleway for 1.2km. Nearing Risley Lodge Farm on the access track, by a sign stating 'no right of way', turn right over a stile on your right, to ascend past the farm (**2**).

Cross several more stiles in the same direction to the highest point where there is a 'trig' point. Emerging on the road by the 'trig' point, turn right for 280m then right again at a public footpath sign. Cross a stile and follow the public footpath across the fields to descend and emerge on the access road to the golf club house by Maywood Farm (**3**).

Cross straight over the access road and onto the golf course, following the white marker posts, descending slightly to a small footbridge. Then following the white marker posts again in the same direction back to the main road. Cross the main road through Risley with care and continue still in the same direction to the A52 dual carriageway (**4**).

The path crosses over the dual carriageway and at the far side, turns left then right and continues a further 1km in the same direction to just before a minor road at Breaston (**5**). Turn right on a narrow public footpath 15m before the road. Continue on that for 1km until you come to a pub called 'The Navigation'.

Cross the road there and continue in the same direction on the former canal route. You come to an access road and signposts to Breaston, Borrowash and Draycott after 300m (**6**), where you turn right and walk up the access road to Cottage Farm (not signposted), a white painted building.

Follow the track turning left behind the farm at the far side then at GR. 454344 behind the farm, bear right across several fields (**7**) for 900m to emerge at a sports field. A row of Tudor design houses may be seen in the distance beside the sports field (**8**).

Emerging on the road by the row of Tudor houses, turn left up Breaston Lane and under the A52. Continue a further 300m to the road junction nearby The Risley Park pub. Turn left to take you back to your starting point.

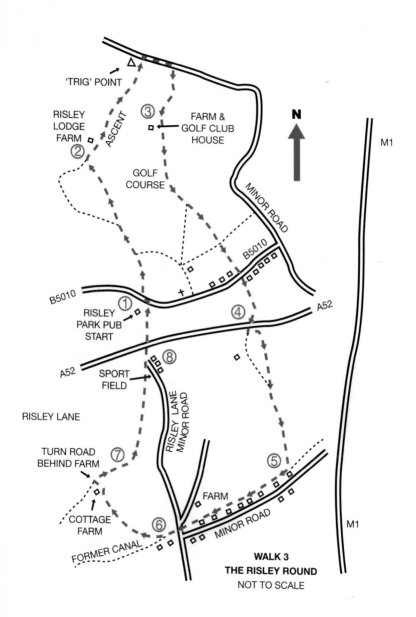

'TRIG' POINT

RISLEY
LODGE
FARM

② ASCENT

③

FARM &
GOLF CLUB
HOUSE

GOLF
COURSE

N

M1

MINOR ROAD

B5010

B5010

RISLEY
PARK PUB
START ①

④

A52

A52

SPORT
FIELD

⑧

RISLEY LANE

RISLEY LANE
MINOR ROAD

TURN ROAD
BEHIND FARM

⑦

⑤

FARM

COTTAGE
FARM

⑥

MINOR ROAD

M1

FORMER CANAL

WALK 3
THE RISLEY ROUND
NOT TO SCALE

Walk 4 The Elvaston Circular   **Distance** 6.2 miles/10 km

Start GR. 409319 At the sharp bend of the road beside The Harrington
Arms pub in Thulston. Park in Brook Road round the corner.

Walk Time 2 hrs 15 mins

Terrain A very nice walk passing ponds, river and the highlight is the
excellent grounds of Elvaston Castle and Country Park. Well worth
the effort.

From Harrington Arms, walk south along the B5010 in Thulston on Broad Lane
to the end of the houses and turn left into Yew Tree Lane. Look for a stile and
opening in Yew Tree Lane on the right (1), leading into a field. Cross and walk
along the edge, keeping the hedge line on your left into the next field. Turn
right and walk straight along the fields keeping the hedge on your right to the
B5010 road.

On reaching the road, turn left, walking on the pavement for 950m to the
entrance to Bellington Farm on the left. Turn along the access road and walk
along the left side of the farm and straight up the field ahead, through the farm
gate. At the next farm gate go through, turn right then left, ascending over the
hillside and through a gate.

You are now on a track between a gravel quarry (2) with some ponds on either
side. Stay on this path for 900m to eventually emerge on a minor road just past
a large pond. Turn left at the road, walking 300m into the village of Ambaston.
Continue straight through the village to the far side.

Turn left at the far end of the village (3); follow a public footpath sign for
Borrowash Bridge by the side of a house. Walk on the Derwent Valley Heritage
Trail now for 800m. Follow the small yellow arrows diagonally right crossing
several fields, and stiles on route.

Look for the way marker posts pointing right through a row of trees to take
you to the riverbank (4) and stay on the path and banking close by the River
Derwent for 2.2km. Continue on the same side of the river, crossing over the
road near a bridge and walk on the riverbank to the obvious waterfall (5).

Turn left as you reach the waterfall on a path, which passes just to the left of a
pylon. Follow this path, which then turns right then left then right then left (6)
parallel with a stream. Ignore other public footpaths on your right and stay on
this main path until you come to a public footpath sign for Elvaston Castle and
Country Park (7).

Turn left at this sign and walk down the track to a small brick bridge and turn
right just before it. Follow the path to another access track signed 'public
bridleway Elvaston'. You pass Elvaston Church and emerge at the large gates
of a former driveway to Elvaston Castle. Turn right at these gates with the
statues at each side and look for a kissing gate diagonally left and public footpath
sign there, just before the avenue of trees (8).

Go through two metal kissing gates and walk on the grass crossing fields then
between the houses to emerge on Brook Road near to where you started.

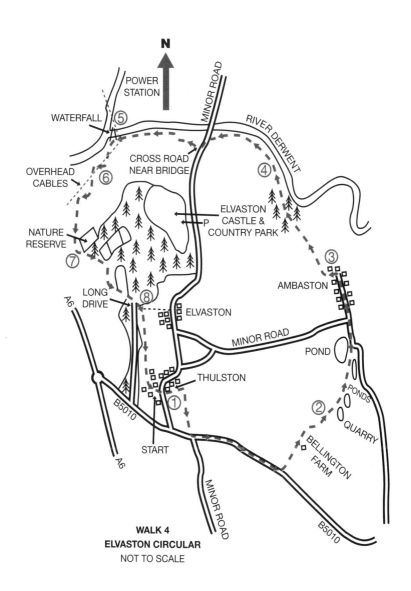

N

POWER
STATION

WATERFALL ⑤

MINOR ROAD

RIVER DERWENT

CROSS ROAD
NEAR BRIDGE

④

OVERHEAD
CABLES ⑥

ELVASTON
CASTLE &
COUNTRY PARK

P

NATURE
RESERVE

⑦

③

AMBASTON

LONG
DRIVE

⑧

ELVASTON

A6

MINOR ROAD

POND

PONDS

THULSTON

①

②

QUARRY

B5010

START

A6

BELLINGTON
FARM

MINOR ROAD

B5010

WALK 4
ELVASTON CIRCULAR
NOT TO SCALE

Walk 5 The Three Woods Walk   **Distance** 6.3 miles/10.1 km
Start GR. 481470 Start from Ram Inn on the B6010 between Beauvale and
Moorgreen near Eastwood.
Walk Time 2 hrs 40 mins
Terrain A good walk and not too strenuous, crossing fields and incorporating
wood, water and open countryside, with a pub stop at the finish.

Leaving from Ram Inn car park, turn left and walk around to the next bend in the
road, and look for a public footpath on your right (1) into a field by a house. Go
through the kissing gate there and follow the worn path straight across two fields
before turning left on a public footpath over fields, to head for the left side of
Greasley Church (2), which you can see on higher ground as you are walking.

Walk past the entrance to the church and through the graveyard to emerge on the
B600 minor road at the far side. Turn right and walk for 200m to a public footpath
on the left side, which is about 50m past Greasley House. Cross the stile there and
ascend the side of the field following the public footpath as it bends right then left
then right and left at the far end of the next field.

Always keep the hedge line on your left as you walk on a general bearing
of 22°M (3) a further 1km over five fields. Ascending the fields, you pass
Brooksbreasting Farm 100m off to your right, just past there; the public footpath
turns right towards the farm entrance.

You emerge on a minor road and turn left, walking for 650m to the corner of a large
forest and a parking area there (4). Turn right and walk along a track towards the
motorway. As you reach the motorway, your track swings round to the left and you
follow the obvious path through the woodland.

You come to a track crossing left to right and you walk straight across still on the
path. Walk a further 530m to a public footpath sign pointing left along the edge of
the forest (5). Follow this all the way anti-clockwise round the edge of the forest
and pick up a track running alongside Moorgreen Reservoir (6). Keep the reservoir
on your right as you follow the obvious path south to the B600 road at the far end.

You emerge at the road junction by Beauvale Lodge. Turn left on the main road
and walk on the pavement for 350m south to a road turning right (7) towards
Moorgreen Industrial Park. Continue past the factories along Engine Lane, in a
straight line for 800m.

As you reach the far end, a sign states height-restricted area and you turn left along
a dismantled railway for 150m then left again behind the factories. After 200m,
turn right, just before a sign for wildlife area (8) to ascend a field keeping the hedge
line to your left.

Go through an opening in the top left of the field and follow the worn path left then
right a further 220m over the hillside to the B6010 road. Turn right on the road and
follow it round for 520m to the second bend and Ram Inn where you started.

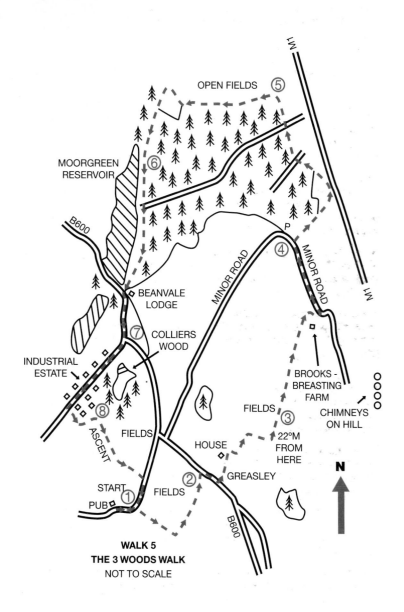

LW

OPEN FIELDS ⑤

MOORGREEN
RESERVOIR

⑥

B600

P

④

MINOR ROAD

MINOR ROAD

LW

BEANVALE
LODGE

⑦ COLLIERS
WOOD

INDUSTRIAL
ESTATE

BROOKS -
BREASTING
FARM

CHIMNEYS
ON HILL

FIELDS ③

22°M
FROM
HERE

⑧

HOUSE

ASCENT

FIELDS

GREASLEY

START ①

PUB

② FIELDS

B600

N

WALK 5
THE 3 WOODS WALK
NOT TO SCALE

Walk 6 Cossall, Strelley & Babbington Walk   **Distance 6.4 miles/10.3 km**
Start GR. 481429 Park and start from the lay-by/telephone box on the main road through Cossall Marsh
Walk Time 2 hrs 45 mins
Terrain A pleasant walk generally over fields with good views and with a pub stop 1/3 way around. Only slightly undulating.

Leaving from the telephone box in Cossall Marsh, ascend the road and walk around the bend. Do not take the first public footpath on your right but continue a short distance to a bridleway on your right beside a large house and gardens. Go through the metal gate there by the sign to Strelley and Trowell and cross the field.

Keep the fence line to your right then cross a small footbridge and ascend the field keeping the hedge on your right as you walk gradually anti-clockwise for 1km before joining a bridleway/access track as you approach Strelley Park Farm (**1**). Bear right towards the farm on the access track and pass the farm on your left, ignoring two public footpaths on your right.

Your path takes you towards a water tower ahead, but first you come to a sign saying private ahead, and you turn left across fields (**2**), bearing 30°M from the turn off, for 500m towards some houses and the water tower. You emerge on a narrow path alongside the houses and walk round and in front of them and on the road past the water tower (**3**).

You emerge beside The Queen Adelaide pub. Walk to the far side of it and turn right on a bridleway between the houses. Look for green arrows on the posts as you soon come to Swingate and continue in front of the houses in a straight line towards the motorway you can hear ahead. Leave the tall mast off to your left (**4**) as you continue straight ahead. A further 700m past the mast, you pass a house on your right as you continue on the access road and over fields in a straight line to the motorway.

Keep the hedge line to your right then as you reach the motorway, turn left to the bridge then right at the far side of it. Walk on the bridleway then minor road for 900m to the church in Strelley. Walk a further 300m to a sharp bend in the road. Turn right here at a metal barrier then left after 80m. Follow the track as it turns right 400m further on.

Your route takes you around Catstone Hill and the underground reservoir on your right (**5**). Continue past it for 190m keeping the hedge line on your right to pass a wood on your right where a public footpath sign for Cossall states 1¼ mile. Turn right here, walking for 500m back to the motorway. Follow the track round and under the motorway.

Continuing on the far side on a general bearing of 303°M for 1.5km in a straight line over several fields until you come to a sharp bend in a road. Turn right and walk down and round the road for 220m. As you ascend to Cossall, halfway up is a short flight of steps on the left (6).

Turn off up the steps and you emerge on the side of the Nottingham Canal. Cross a footbridge in front of you and turn right on the towpath, keeping the canal on your right side (7). Continue for approx. 2km until you reach the factories and a bridge over the road at Cossall Marsh.

Cross the bridge and look for a flight of steps on the left, descending to the road below. On reaching the road, turn left to take you back to your start point 220m further.

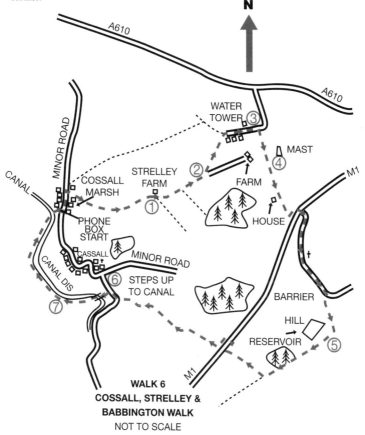

WALK 6
COSSALL, STRELLEY &
BABBINGTON WALK
NOT TO SCALE

Walk 7 The Two Canals Circular   **Distance 6.5 miles/10.5 km**
Start GR. 481429 Park and start from the lay-by/telephone box on the main road through Cossall Marsh. Take care walking with children by the side of the canal!
Walk Time 2 hrs 30 mins
Terrain A virightually flat walk but interesting along the towpaths and footpaths with varied wildlife to see on route.

Leaving from the junction of Coronation Road and Church Lane 100m from the telephone box (1) at Cossall Marsh, walk towards Ilkeston and under the two concrete bridges then turn right onto the public footpath signed Newton's Lane and Awsworth. This takes you up a flight of steps onto the Nottingham Canal towpath.

Keep left on the towpath and stay on it for 1.5km, keeping the canal on your right (2). On route you cross two roads. Eventually the canal stops and your path bears round to the left through a wooded area (3). Follow it round and across a disused road then the path turns sharp left for 400m by bushes and trees.

You cross a stream and continue on the obvious path through open fields. Where the path divides soon after crossing the stream, keep on the path straight-ahead heading for the church tower. You come to a green sign stating Bridleway Eastwood to the left. Turn left here (4) and continue, nearby a busy road until you come to a minor road ahead (5).

On reaching the minor road, turn left, walking for 450m over the River Erewash to the Erewash Canal 140m further. Stay on the towpath for 4.3km, heading in a general southerly direction keeping the canal on your right and crossing under a railway bridge and three roads on route (one newly built).

After crossing under the third road, continue for 900m (looking for the footbridge over the railway), to some lock gates near the railway line on your left (6). Walk a further 50m then turn left along a path to a footbridge over the railway lines. Cross it and ascend for 360m back to the Nottingham Canal. Turn left on the towpath (7) and walk for 1.1km back to the original start point at Cossall Marsh.

Turn left just past the factory units as you approach Cossall Marsh and descend the steps again, back to the minor road. Turn left again on the road to take you back to your original start point.

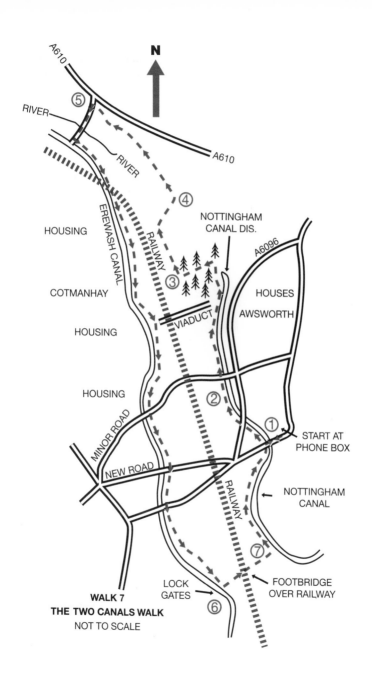

N

A610

A610

⑤

RIVER

RIVER

EREWASH CANAL

HOUSING

COTMANHAY

HOUSING

HOUSING

MINOR ROAD

NEW ROAD

④

RAILWAY

③

NOTTINGHAM
CANAL DIS.

A6096

HOUSES

AWSWORTH

VIADUCT

②

①

START AT
PHONE BOX

NOTTINGHAM
CANAL

RAILWAY

⑦

LOCK
GATES

⑥

FOOTBRIDGE
OVER RAILWAY

WALK 7
THE TWO CANALS WALK
NOT TO SCALE

Walk 8 The Mapperley Round   **Distance 7.2 miles/11.6 km**
Start GR. 435422 Park/start near to junction of A609 & minor road to Mapperley near Coppice Farm.
Walk Time 4 hrs
Terrain A pleasant walk over fields and through Shipley Country Park. Some good views from Shipley Hill especially, as you pass American Adventure.

Walk along the minor road to pass Coppice Farm on your left. 100 m past the farm, turn left (**1**), crossing a stile on the left into a field and follow the public footpath across the field in the direction of woodland. You cross stiles into three fields then in the fourth field; you bear right to pick up a worn path (**2**) between the hedges on each side. On reaching this path, turn left.

Look for a yellow arrow on a post a short distance further. When you see this, turn right on a narrow concealed path through the bushes and over the stream and stile into a field. Turn left, keeping the hedge line to your left and go through a metal kissing gate. Continue to a minor road (**3**), cross and soon after go through a kissing gate.

Follow the worn path round the edge of a copse and cross a stile into a field. Walk straight across the field, passing a large tree in the middle, as you continue in the same direction to the next hedge line. Head in the same direction towards a ruined farm ahead at GR. 418427 (**4**). Cross two stiles together and walk on an access track to the left of the farm.

You come to a bend in the track, but walk straight ahead as you go under the electricity cables, do not turn left. Head towards the left of a wood ahead and turn right at the far end. Walk between the fence on both sides and cross a stile then turn left. Walk along the field and go over a stile at the yellow arrow. Continue straight ahead over several fields and stiles keeping the hedge on your left.

You continue to a public footpath sign pointing left then turn immediately right and walk between the hedge and a wire fence on a narrow path. You cross several stiles to emerge on a bridge and access road (**5**). Turn right, walking for 2.9km in a general easterly direction on the access road to a minor road and entrance to Shipley Country Park (**6**).

Walk up the entrance road of Shipley Country Park into the wooded area and continue clockwise all the way round the access road, then track as you pass Shipley Hall at the far side. Continue clockwise and look for a small post with yellow arrow pointing left down the hill then turn left immediately again (**7**) to take you to an access track then right descending to nearby Shipley Lake at American Adventure.

Continue round to a sign and a path junction pointing right on cycle route 67 and follow this. Soon after it turns left on route 67 again. You come to a sign saying Nutbrook Trail ahead. Follow this until you come to a small bridge overhead (**8**) and a muddy path just before it on the right at GR. 449426.

Turn right before the bridge and walk up onto an access track going straight ahead.

Stay on it for 600m until you come to an access road and small parking area. Turn left on the access road and walk along to the A609 to emerge beside the Newdigate pub (**9**). Turn right on the main road and walk for 700m back to the lane near where you started. Turn right again to take you back to your star point.

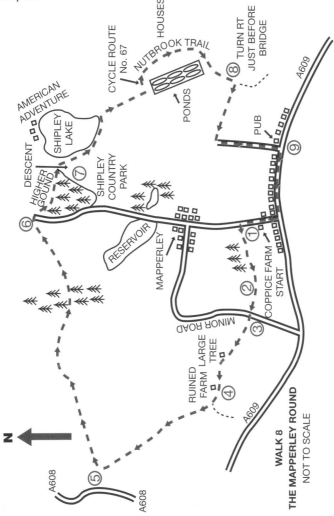

WALK 8
THE MAPPERLEY ROUND
NOT TO SCALE

Walk 9 River Trent View Circular   **Distance** 8.8 miles/14.1km
Start GR. 545344 The Crusader Pub at Clifton
Walk Time 4 hrs
Terrain A pleasant walk initially over fields then through woods before crossing fields again nearby the River Trent.

Leaving from beside the Crusader pub, cross the road onto Nottingham Road (1) and walk in a generally southerly direction, passing Farnborough Road to the end of the houses on the left side at GR. 544334.

Go through a kissing gate on your left at the end of the houses on Nottingham Road (2). Look for a small copse in the field and walk to the right of it then to the left of the large wood in the distance. On the way across the fields you will cross three small footbridges.

The path emerges back on the main road where you turn left for 150m and walk along to a public footpath sign on the right, pointing along an access road near a bungalow (3). Follow this to the far end of the lane then cross the step stile on your left, which leads up to the wood. The path ascends the left side of the wood.

Go through a gate as you ascend then the path sweeps round clockwise near the top. At the top there is a kissing gate to your right and a metal walkers gate and bridleway sign on the left. Go through the left gate (4), following the blue arrow and continue along Gotham Hill to the next wood called Gotham Hill Wood.

You arrive at a kissing gate on your right at the start of the wood. Cross then follow a long straight flat path through the woods to the far end. Arriving at an opening in a fence 800m further on (5), turn right to descend the hillside between the woods. Go through a walker's gate near the bottom and walk past a bungalow.

Just past the bungalow, turn left along the access track, which takes you along to the main A453 road. Cross with extreme care and look for the opening leading into the village of Thrumpton. Continue straight along the lane to the church in Thrumpton (6) then follow it round to the entrance to Thrumpton Hall. The road bends right there then left, heading to the river.

On reaching the river, keep right along the path nearby and over a series of fields. The path crosses a cattle grid then bears right across the fields. You can see two church spires and you walk across the fields towards the right one at Barton in Fabis. Nearing the village, walk round a large pond (7) and into the village and past the church.

Follow Manor Road as it turns right then left then right again. Turn left 170m further, past the last buildings to walk along the bottom of Brandshill Wood (8) and still broadly in line with the river in the same direction as previous.

Continue on the lower ground for 1.8km to Holme Pit Nature Reserve (**9**) and then in the same direction a further 500m to a public footpath sign and path ascending right. Follow this path past the university building and car park. Where the road bends left a short distance further, take the right fork and walk along the footpath for 500m onto the main A453 road through Clifton. Turn right on the road and continue for 400m to your starting point.

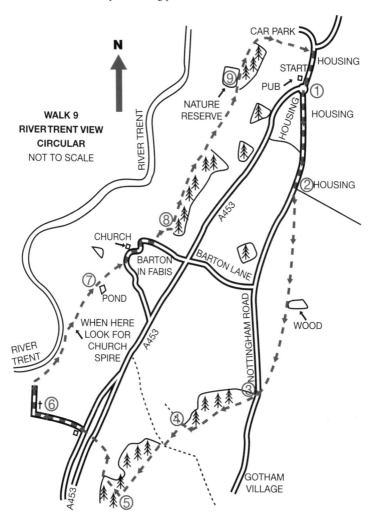

Notes